THE YELLOW WALLPAPER

Charlotte Perkins Gilman

AUTHORED by Teddy Wayne
UPDATED AND REVISED by Caitlin Vincent

COVER DESIGN by Table XI Partners LLC
COVER PHOTO by Olivia Verma and © 2005 GradeSaver, LLC

BOOK DESIGN by Table XI Partners LLC

Published by GradeSaver LLC, www.gradesaver.com

First published in the United States of America by GradeSaver LLC. 2002

GRADESAVER, the GradeSaver logo and the phrase "Getting you the grade since 1999" are registered trademarks of GradeSaver, LLC

ISBN 978-1-60259-163-9

Printed in the United States of America

For other products and additional information please visit
http://www.gradesaver.com

Table of Contents

Table of Contents

Biography of Charlotte Perkins Gilman (1860-1935)

Charlotte Perkins Gilman was born Charlotte Anna Perkins on July 3, 1860, in Hartford, Connecticut. The youngest child and only daughter of Frederick Perkins and Mary Ann Fitch Westcott, Gilman was also the great-niece of 19th-century writer Harriet Beecher Stowe (author of "Uncle Tom's Cabin"). After two of Gilman's siblings died, her mother was told not to have any other children, and Gilman's father abandoned them shortly afterward. Without the support of their father, Gilman and her family were left in a state of extreme poverty and were forced to move from relative to relative in Rhode Island in order to survive. After her father's departure, Gilman's mother grew increasingly cold and detached, striving to protect her children from suffering by denying them affection. Without the desire for affection from others, she believed, Gilman and her siblings would be self-reliant and emotionally independent.

Lacking a father's presence or mother's affection, Gilman often retreated to the public library to overcome her loneliness. She spent much of her time studying ancient civilizations and reading texts about philosophy and historical development. She also became friends with the families of Eli Whitney Blake, Jeremiah Lewis Diman, William F. Channing, Rowland Hazard, and Edward Everett Hale, each of whom had intellectual significance in the area. She only received limited formal education in public schools and mostly educated herself with her extensive reading.

In 1878, Gilman enrolled in the Rhode Island School of Design, supporting herself as a tutor and an artist of trade cards. In 1883, Gilman published her first works, sending articles and poems to the "Providence Journal," the "Woman's Journal," "The Century," and the "Christian Register." In 1884, Gilman consented to marry Charles Walter Stetson, a handsome aspiring artist who had courted her intensely the previous year. Three months after their marriage, Gilman learned that she was pregnant and began to suffer from some symptoms of depression.

After the birth of her daughter, Katharine, in 1885, Gilman became overwhelmed with depression and began treatment with Dr. Silas Weir Mitchell, a prominent physician who favored the "rest cure" for the treatment of nervous disorders. Although Gilman attempted to adhere to Mitchell's prescriptions, she was unable to tolerate the treatment for more than a few months. Gilman later satirized the treatment in "The Yellow Wallpaper," which she published in 1892.

In 1888 Gilman separated from Stetson and moved to California. The couple divorced in 1894, and Gilman ultimately sent her daughter to be raised by Stetson and his new wife. During her time in California, Gilman became extremely active in social reform, particularly the suffrage movement. She also began to write prolifically, publishing fifteen essays, numerous poems, and a novella in 1890. Gilman's first volume of poems, "In This World," published in 1893, first brought her public recognition from a literary perspective. Her book, "Women and Economics" (1898) won her international recognition.

After the death of her mother, Gilman returned to the East Coast and married Houghton Gilman, her first cousin, in 1900. Her second marriage was much more successful than her first, and Gilman continued to write numerous works, including: "The Home: Its Work and Influence" (1903), "What Diantha Did" (1910), "The Crux" (1911), "Moving the Mountain" (1911), and the utopian text "Herland" (1915). Gilman also began to write her autobiography, "The Living of Charlotte Perkins Gilman" in 1925.

In 1932, Gilman was diagnosed with incurable breast cancer. After her husband died suddenly in 1934, Gilman moved back to California to live near her daughter. In 1935, she committed suicide with an overdose of chloroform, writing in her suicide note that she "chose chloroform over cancer." Her autobiography was published posthumously.

After her death until the middle of the 1950s, Gilman largely disappeared from the world of literary scholarship. If anything, historians merely highlighted Gilman as a figure of the suffrage movement, and failed to recognize her literary achievements on a serious level. Gilman finally began to receive recognition for her work with the women's movement and development of feminist scholarship in the 1960s and 1970s. In the past two decades, Gilman has become particularly well-known for "Herland" and "The Yellow Wallpaper," both of which have achieved prominent positions in the canon of contemporary literature. Gilman's legacy is still being uncovered today, as much of her previously neglected work is currently being republished.

About The Yellow Wallpaper

"The Yellow Wallpaper" is an exaggerated account of Charlotte Perkins Gilman's personal experiences. In 1887, shortly after the birth of her daughter, Gilman began to suffer from serious depression and fatigue. She was referred to Silas Weir Mitchell, a leading specialist in women's nervous disorders in the nineteenth century, who diagnosed Gilman with neurasthenia and prescribed a "rest cure" of forced inactivity. Weir Mitchell believed that nervous depression was a result of overactive nerves and ordered Gilman to cease all forms of creative activity, including writing, for the rest of her life. The goal of the treatment was to promote domesticity and calm her agitated nerves.

Gilman attempted to endure the "rest cure" treatment and did not write or work for three months. Eventually, she felt herself beginning to go slowly insane from the inactivity and, at one point, was reduced to crawling under her bed holding a rag doll. Unlike the protagonist in her story, Gilman did not reach the point of total madness, but she knew that her deteriorating mental condition was due to the oppressive medical regime that was meant to "cure" her. She abandoned Mitchell's advice and moved to California in order to overcome her depression on her own. Although Gilman's attempt was successful, she claimed to suffer from post-traumatic stress from Weir Mitchell's treatment for the rest of her life. In 1890, Gilman wrote "The Yellow Wallpaper" in an effort to save other women from suffering the same oppressive treatment. Weir Mitchell and his treatment play a key role in the narrative; in the third section of the text, the protagonist's husband even threatens to send her to Weir Mitchell in the fall if she does not recover soon.

In 1890, Gilman sent the story to writer William Dean Howells, who submitted it to Horace Scudder, editor of the prestigious magazine, "The Atlantic Monthly." Scudder rejected the story as depressing material, and returned it to Gilman with a handwritten note that read: "Dear Madam: W. Howells has handed me this story. I could not forgive myself if I made others as miserable as I have made myself! Sincerely Yours, H. E. Scudder." Eventually the story was published in "The New England Magazine" in May 1892. According to Gilman's autobiography, she sent a copy of "The Yellow Wallpaper" to Weir Mitchell after its publication. Although she never received a response, she claimed that Weir Mitchell later changed his official treatment for nervous depression as a direct result of her story. Gilman also asserted that she knew of one particular woman who had been spared the "rest cure" as a treatment for her depression after her family read "The Yellow Wallpaper."

The public reaction to the story was strong, if mixed. In many circles, "The Yellow Wallpaper" was perceived as nothing more than a horror story, stemming from the gothic example of Edgar Allen Poe and Mary Shelley. It was not until the 1970s that the story was also recognized as a feminist narrative worthy of historical and literary scholarship.

Character List

Narrator

Modeled after Charlotte Perkins Gilman, the narrator in "The Yellow Wallpaper" is a young wife and mother who has recently began to suffer symptoms of depression and anxiety. Although she does not believe that anything is wrong with her, John, her physician husband, diagnoses her with neurasthenia and prescribes several months of S. Weir Mitchell's famed "rest cure." In addition to being confined to the nursery in their rented summer home, the narrator is expressly forbidden to write or engage in any creative activity. The narrator desperately wants to please her husband and assume her role as an ideal mother and wife, but she is unable to balance her husband's needs with her desire to express her creativity. While attempting to adhere to John's wishes for the most part, the narrator secretly writes in her journal, seeking solace from her extreme loneliness and inactivity. Over the course of the story, the narrator also begins to find comfort in the hideous yellow wallpaper that covers the walls of the nursery. She gradually begins to see a female figure trapped behind the bar-like pattern of the wallpaper and realizes that both she and the figure are suffering from oppression and imprisonment. As the narrator becomes more and more preoccupied with the pattern of the wallpaper, she forgets her desire to become the perfect wife and mother and thinks only of a way to release the imprisoned woman from the wallpaper. Gilman's increasingly choppy prose and disjointed stream-of-consciousness express the narrator's growing insanity with each passing day. By the end of the story, the narrator has lost all sense of reality, and John discovers her creeping around the perimeter of the nursery, following the endless pattern of the wallpaper. While she discards her duty as a wife and mother, as well as her sanity, the narrator ultimately triumphs in her personal quest to release the woman in the wallpaper - and thus liberates herself.

In some editions of the story, the narrator declares her liberation from the wallpaper and the rational world by proclaiming, "I've got out at last...in spite of you and Jane." Some scholars argue that "Jane" is simply a misprint for "Jennie," John's sister and housekeeper. Yet, it is also possible that "Jane" is the actual name of the narrator, a character who remains a nameless stereotype of female social oppression for the entirely of the story. If this "Jane" is, in fact, the narrator, then Gilman suggests that the narrator's liberation from sanity and the bars of the wallpaper also means an "escape" from her own sense of self.

John

The husband of the narrator, John is a practical physician who believes that his wife is suffering from nothing more than a "slight hysterical tendency." He prescribes the "rest cure," confining the narrator to the nursery and forbidding her to exercise her creative imagination in any way. His antagonism toward her imagination stems from his own rationality and personal anxiety about creativity;

he scoffs openly at the narrator's fancies and is incapable of understanding her true nature. Throughout the story, he treats her in an infantile manner, referring to her as his "blessed little goose" and "little girl." Moreover, when the narrator attempts to discuss her unhappiness with the situation in a mature manner, he refuses to accept her as an equal and simply carries her back up to the nursery for more bed rest. He is fixed in his authoritative position as husband and doctor and cannot adapt his strategy to account for her opinion on the matter. He believes in a strict, paternalistic divide between men and women; men work outside of the home, as he does, while women like Jennie, his sister, and Mary, the nanny, tend to the house.

Although John is set up as the villain of the story, he can also be seen as a more sympathetic character. He clearly loves his wife and relies on her for his own happiness. Yet he is unable to reconcile her creative desires with his own rationality or the chauvinistic expectations of the time period. His wife is unable or unwilling to adhere to the ideal model of domesticity expressed by the 19th-century society, and John is at a loss as to what to do. His solution is to use Weir Mitchell's rest cure to "fix" his wife, and he does not realize that his own actions push her over the edge of insanity.

Woman in the wallpaper

Although the narrator eventually believes that she sees many women in the yellow wallpaper, she centers on one in particular. The woman appears to be trapped within the bar-like pattern of the wallpaper, and she shakes the pattern as she tries to break out. The woman is most active by moonlight, a symbol of femininity and a sign that John's strict daytime regimen is no longer applicable to the narrator.

Over time, as the narrator's insanity deepens, she identifies completely with this woman and believes that she, too, is trapped within the wallpaper. As a ghostly counterpart of the narrator, the woman in the wallpaper also symbolizes female imprisonment within the domestic sphere. Unable to break free from the room, like the narrator, the woman in the wallpaper has only the symbolic option of tending to the house as a wife or mother. The woman's habit of "creeping" suggests that she must still be secretive after she has achieved her liberation. Social norms will not accept her freedom from the domestic sphere, and so she must creep furtively and lie in wait in the shadows of the wallpaper.

Jennie

Jennie is the narrator's sister-in-law and takes care of the house during the narrator's illness. Although she does not play an active role in the narrative, she is a constant reminder of the narrator's inability to assume her proper role as John's wife and housekeeper. Always maintaining a passive position under John's supervision, Jennie symbolizes the happily domesticated woman who does not find anything wrong with her domestic prison. However, Gilman also suggests that there may be more to Jennie than meets the eye: the narrator acknowledges that

Jennie is aware of the narrator's growing interest in the wallpaper and even discusses her future with John.

Mary

Mary takes care of the narrator and John's baby. With her name a possible allusion to the Virgin Mary, Mary is the perfect mother-surrogate for the narrator, an idealized maternal figure whose only concern is her child. Like Jennie, she also symbolizes the happily domesticated woman. Although Mary is even less present in the text than Jennie, she still serves to remind the narrator of her personal failings as a 19th century woman, particularly in terms of her own child.

Major Themes

The Yellow Wallpaper

In the story, wallpaper, a usually feminine, floral decoration on the interior of walls, is a symbol of female imprisonment within the domestic sphere. Over the course of the story, the wallpaper becomes a text of sorts through which the narrator exercises her literary imagination and identifies with a feminist double figure.

When John curbs her creativity and writing, the narrator takes it upon herself to make some sense of the wallpaper. She reverses her initial feeling of being watched by the wallpaper and starts actively studying and decoding its meaning. She untangles its chaotic pattern and locates the figure of a woman struggling to break free from the bars in the pattern. Over time, as her insanity deepens, she identifies completely with this woman and believes that she, too, is trapped within the wallpaper. When she tears down the wallpaper over her last couple of nights, she believes that she has finally broken out of the wallpaper within which John has imprisoned her. The wallpaper's yellow color has many possible associations - with jaundiced sickness, with discriminated-against minorities of the time (especially the Chinese), and with the rigid oppression of masculine sunlight. By tearing it down, the narrator emerges from the wallpaper and asserts her own identity, albeit a somewhat confused, insane one. Though she must crawl around the room, as the woman in the wallpaper crawls around, this "creeping" is the first stage in a feminist uprising.

Creativity vs. Rationality

From the beginning of the story, the narrator's creativity is set in conflict with John's rationality. As a writer, the narrator thrives in her use of her imagination, and her creativity is an inherent part of her nature. John does not recognize his wife's fundamental creativity and believes that he can force out her imaginative fancies and replace them with his own solid rationality. In essence, a large part of the "rest cure" focuses on John's attempt to remove the narrator's creativity; by forcing her to give up her writing, he hopes that he will calm her anxious nature and help her to assume her role as an ideal wife and mother.

However, the narrator is not able to suppress her creativity, despite her best efforts to follow John's instructions. Because she is not able to write openly and feels the repression of her imagination, she inadvertently exercises her mind via the yellow wallpaper. Although the narrator attempts to incorporate John's rationality into the chaotic pattern of the wallpaper, she fails; the wallpaper cannot be quantified in John's way. Her repressed imagination takes control, and she loses all sense of reality, becoming lost in delusions and the idea that she herself was the woman trapped in the wallpaper.

Gilman believes in creativity without restraints and argues that the narrator's repressed imagination is the fundamental cause of her psychotic breakdown. Gilman also suggests that the narrator's attempt to deny a fundamental part of her nature was doomed from the beginning. John should have been able to accept the true nature of his wife, rather than trying to force her to adhere to the prescriptions of his own personality.

The Domestic Sphere as Prison

Throughout the story, Gilman presents the domestic sphere as a prison for the narrator. Just as the woman in the wallpaper is trapped behind a symbol of the feminine domestic sphere, the narrator is trapped within the prison-like nursery. The nursery is itself a symbol of the narrator's oppression as a constant reminder of her duty to clean the house and take care of the children. The numerous barred windows and immovable bed also suggest a more malignant use for the nursery in the past, perhaps as a room used to house an insane person. The narrator's sense of being watched by the wallpaper accentuates the idea of the room as a surveillance-friendly prison cell.

John's treatment of the narrator perpetuates this sense of the domestic sphere as a prison. As a practical doctor, John automatically patronizes his imaginative, literary wife. He views her writing as unimportant, rarely takes her anxieties seriously, and constantly refers to her with the diminutive "little." The narrator has no option of escaping her role as a wife and mother; John is unable to perceive her as anything more than that. However, the narrator is imprisoned even further because Jennie and Mary assume her identity as wife and mother; the narrator has no identity left to her because even the ones provided by the society have been taken from her. Unlike the narrator, Mary and Jennie do not have any aspirations beyond the prison of the domestic sphere and thus, they do not recognize it as a prison at all.

The "Rest Cure"

Because of Gilman's personal experience with the "rest cure," it is not surprising that S. Weir Mitchell's treatment plays a significant role in the context of the narrative. From the start of the story, the narrator is supposed to be suffering from neurasthenia, a disease that requires Weir Mitchell's particular technique for nervousness. Yet, it is unclear if the narrator is actually ill, or if the "rest cure" treatment causes her to go insane. Gilman's argument is that a treatment that requires complete inactivity is ultimately far more detrimental to a woman suffering from a minor anxiety disorder. Significantly, according to Gilman's autobiography, she sent a copy of "The Yellow Wallpaper" to Weir Mitchell, and he subsequently changed his treatment for neurasthenia.

Beyond the "rest cure," Gilman also criticizes any sort of medical treatment in which the personal opinion of the patient is not considered. Although the narrator repeatedly asks John to change the treatment over the course of the story, he refuses to acknowledge her requests, believing that he had total authority over the situation. This is also a reflection of the society conditions of the time, but either way, John abuses his power as both a husband and physician and forces the narrator to remain in an oppressive situation from which her only escape is insanity.

Role of Women in the 19th Century

According to the social norms of the time period, women in the 19th century were expected to fulfill their duties as wives and mothers and be content in their existence as nothing more. Men and women were divided between the public and private sphere, and women were doomed to spend their lives solely in the domestic sphere. Not coincidentally, women who dared to enter the masculine public realm were viewed as something akin to prostitutes, the lowest level of society.

With that in mind, although John could be seen as the domineering villain of the story, he is simply a reflection of his society. The narrator's desire to have more in her life than John and her child does not correspond to social expectations. Moreover, her love of writing and creativity further distinguishes her from the idealized "angel of the house" that she is supposed to emulate. Gilman herself rebelled against these social expectations and, by leaving her first husband and moving to California to write, was not deemed fit to belong in respectable society.

The Narrator vs. The Woman in the Wallpaper

From the start, the narrator has a constant bond with the woman in the wallpaper. Even when the narrator is unable to discern her figure beyond the pattern, she is still preoccupied with the wallpaper and feels an uncanny connection to it. As the story continues, the narrator's connection to the woman in the wallpaper is heightened, and Gilman begins to present the wallpaper woman as a sort of doppelganger to the narrator. Although the woman is trapped behind the chaotic yellow wallpaper, she is essentially in the same position as the narrator: imprisoned in the domestic sphere and unable to escape without being strangled by the bars of social expectation.

By the end of the narrative, the narrator's insanity has reached such a heightened state that she can no longer differentiate herself from the figure that she has seen in the wallpaper. She is the woman in the wallpaper and no one, not even John, can imprison her in the wallpaper again. There is no doubt that the narrator will be physically imprisoned at some point in the future. After John regains consciousness and discovers his wife still creeping around the nursery, he will have no choice but to send her to Weir Mitchell or place her in a mental institution. Yet, the narrator's mind will still remain "free," mirroring the freedom enjoyed by the woman in the wallpaper. In other words, the woman in the wallpaper can be seen as a manifestation of her creative imagination that finally breaks through the rigid expectations of the domestic sphere. Unfortunately, the escape of her imagination means that she cannot ever regain any sort of rationality; by freeing the woman in the wallpaper, the narrator ensures that her mind will be . trapped in a prison of insanity.

Sunlight vs. Moonlight

Although the yellow color of the wallpaper has associations with illness, its most developed motif is the conflict between sunlight and moonlight. In Gilman's story, sunlight is associated with John's ordered, dominating schedule and the rational sphere of men. John prescribes something for the narrator for every waking hour while he goes about his daily rounds, forcing her to take on the same order and control that defines his life.

At night, however, the balance shifts. Men's day jobs in the public sphere are irrelevant, and women can achieve a more equal level with their husbands. While he is asleep, John is unable to monitor the narrator's behavior, and she is not in a perpetual state of inferiority or being constantly controlled. More importantly, the narrator's flexible subconscious roams free at night, as in during dreams. It is always by moonlight, a traditional symbol of femininity and the Goddess Artemis, that the narrator understands more about the figure trapped within the wallpaper. In sunlight, the woman stays still, afraid of being caught, and, once she creeps about outside, she does so boldly only at night. Moreover, the narrator cannot see the figure under the oppressive glare of sunlight in her room and is overwhelmed by the pattern of the wallpaper. By the cool, feminine light of the moon, the narrator is able to grasp the woman's plight and ultimately recognize in it a reflection of her own imprisonment.

Glossary of Terms

ancestral

relating to or inherited from an ancestor or pre-existing group

arabesque

an elaborate spiraling line or motif

arbor

a latticework shelter intertwined with vines and leaves

atrocious

dreadful or revolting; extremely tasteless

bloated

swollen or puffed

breadth

width

bulbous

bulging roundness

canvas

a woven cloth of linen or cotton

chintz

a printed cotton fabric

companionship

fellowship between two individuals

congenial

pleasant or agreeable

conscientiously

meticulously or carefully

conspicuous

obvious or easily noticed

convolution

a shape made up of coiling and rolling curves

creep

to move slowly, close to the ground; often on hands and knees

cultivate

to encourage the growth or development of something

debase

to reduce in terms of value and significance

defiance

to challenge or strive to resist

delirium tremens

a phrase literally meaning "shaking delirium" or "trembling madness"

derision

mocking scorn or contempt

draught

the British form of the term "draft," meaning "a current of air"

enduring

lasting

fancy

a fantasy or illusion

felicity

happiness

flamboyant

marked by elaborate curves and decorations

florid

ornate or elaborate

flourish

an embellishment or additional ornament

fretful

restless or irritable

frieze

an ornamented band on furniture or architecture

fungus

a spore-producing organism that decomposes and absorbs the material surrounding it

galore

plentiful

gnarly

full of knots

gouge

to create a hole by chiseling or scooping

grotesque

bizarre or atypical

hedge

a dense row of low shrubs

hereditary

passed from parent to offspring

hovering

suspended over an object or area

hysterical

emotional excitability and mental disturbance; from the Greek word "hystera" meaning "uterus"

impertinence

being insolent or inappropriate

impressionable

easily affected

inanimate

not alive

infuriating

causing outrage or anger

inharmonious

conflicting or incompatible

interminable

endless

lease

rent

loll

to droop or hang

lurid

shining with an unnatural and ghastly glow

neglect

to disregard

nervous

easily excited; characterized by overly-sensitive nerves

neurasthenia

a psychological disorder characterized by nervous exhaustion

odor

smell

optic

visual

peculiarity

oddity

perplexing

confusingly complicated

perseverance

persistence or hard work in the face of obstacles

phosphate

a form of phosphoric acid used for medical treatments

piazza

porch

plantain

a plant from the genus Plantago, characterized by large, oval leaves

plunge

to throw oneself violently forward

provoke

to cause or stimulate purposefully

queer

odd

querulous

whining or complaining

radiate

to extend or spread from a central point

ravage

to damage seriously

recurrent

appearing again or periodically

renovate

to restore or revive

repellent

repulsive; arousing disgust

reproachful

disapproving

restrained

held back or reserved in emotions and behavior

riotous

enthusiastic and boisterous

Romanesque

relating to an architectural style popular in Europe between the 9th and 12the centuries; characterized by arches, columns, and ornamentation

scoff

to mock

skulk

to move sneakily

smooch

a smudge

smouldering

to exist in a state of suppressed activity

spite

hatred or malice

sprawling

spread out awkwardly

stimulus

something that causes action or emotion

stir

to move slightly

subdued

lacking in strength or intensity

sulphur

the British form of the term "sulfur," meaning "greenish-yellow"

temperament

the mental, physical, and emotional qualities that make up an individual

tint

a lighter shade of a color; hue

tonic

a medicine meant to strengthen and invigorate

trample

to stamp or step on heavily

untenanted

not currently occupied or leased by a tenant

vicious

savage or spiteful

waddle

to move awkwardly

wallow

to roll or flounder in a clumsy manner

wharf

a dock or pier

whim

a sudden desire or turn of mind

whitewash

to whiten with whitewash, a liquid composition of water, lime, and whiting

Short Summary

The narrator and her physician husband, John, have rented a mansion for the summer so that she can recuperate from a "slight hysterical tendency." Although the narrator does not believe that she is actually ill, John is convinced that she is suffering from "neurasthenia" and prescribes the "rest cure" treatment. She is confined to bed rest in a former nursery room and is forbidden from working or writing. The spacious, sunlit room has yellow wallpaper – stripped off in two places – with a hideous, chaotic pattern. The narrator detests the wallpaper, but John refuses to change rooms, arguing that the nursery is best-suited for her recovery.

Two weeks later, the narrator's condition has worsened. She feels a constant sense of anxiety and fatigue and can barely muster enough energy to write in her secret journal. Fortunately, their nanny, Mary, takes care of their baby, and John's sister, Jennie, is a perfect housekeeper. The narrator's irritation with the wallpaper grows; she discovers a recurring pattern of bulbous eyes and broken necks, as well as the faint image of a skulking figure stuck behind the pattern.

As more days pass, the narrator grows increasingly anxious and depressed. The wallpaper provides her only stimulation, and she spends the majority of her time studying its confusing patterns which, as she asserts, are almost as "good as gymnastics." The image of the figure stooping down and "creeping" around behind the wallpaper becomes clearer each day. By moonlight, she can see very distinctly that the figure is a woman trapped behind bars. The narrator attempts to convince John to leave the house for a visit with relatives, but he refuses, and the narrator does not feel comfortable confiding in him about her discoveries in the wallpaper. Moreover, she is becoming paranoid that John and Jennie are also interested in the wallpaper and is determined that only she will uncover its secrets.

The narrator's health improves as her interest in the wallpaper deepens. She suspects that Jennie and John are observing her behavior, but her only concern is that they become obstacles to her and the wallpaper. She also begins to notice that the distinct "yellow smell" of the wallpaper has spread over the house, following her even when she goes for rides. At night, the woman in the wallpaper shakes the bars in the pattern violently as she tries to break through them, but she cannot break free. The swirling pattern has strangled the heads of the many women who have tried to break through the wallpaper. The narrator begins to hallucinate, believing that she has seen the woman creeping surreptitiously outside in the sunlight. The narrator intends to peel off the wallpaper before she leaves the house in two days.

That night, the narrator helps the woman in the wallpaper by peeling off the wallpaper halfway around the room. The next day, Jennie is shocked, but the narrator convinces her that she only stripped the wallpaper out of spite. Jennie is able to understand the desire to peel off the ugly wallpaper and does not tell John that anything is out of the ordinary. The next night, the narrator locks herself in her room and continues stripping the wallpaper. She hears shrieks within the wallpaper as she tears it off. She contemplates jumping out of a window, but the bars prevent that; besides, she is afraid of all of the women that are creeping about outside of the house. When morning comes, the narrator has peeled off all of the wallpaper and begun to creep around the perimeter of the room. John eventually breaks into the room, but the narrator does not recognize him. She informs him that she has peeled off most of the wallpaper so that now no one can put her back inside the walls. John faints, and the narrator continues creeping around the room over him.

Summary and Analysis of Part 1

The anonymous female narrator and her physician husband, John, have rented out a colonial mansion for the summer. The narrator is immediately awed by the majestic beauty of the house and considers herself lucky to be able to spend the summer living there. However, she still finds "something queer" about the house. John hopes that the change of scenery and absence from city life will help the narrator recover from a "slight hysterical tendency." John, a practical man, does not believe that the narrator is actually sick and decides that the best cure for her nervousness is the "rest cure," a treatment promoted by the famous physician, S. Weir Mitchell.

John gives the narrator tonics and medicines to help with her recovery, but primarily directs her to stop writing. According to Weir Mitchell's theory, any sort of creative activity will have a detrimental effect on the patient. The narrator does not agree with this part of her treatment and hates not being allowed to write while she rests; she suspects that work would actually speed her recovery. She has been writing occasionally in a small journal, but it is exhausting to do so in secret. The narrator also believes that her condition would improve if she were allowed to have more company. However, John tells her that such stimulation will only aggravate her nervousness.

John outlines a specific daily regimen for the narrator to follow, especially when he is in town seeing patients. He portions out every hour of the day in careful precision, ensuring that she will get plenty of rest without the chance to exercise her creativity.

The narrator discusses the house and its beautiful surroundings. The house is solitary, has hedges and walls and gates, smaller houses for gardeners and other workers, and an elegant garden. Still, she feels there is something strange about the house. She attempts to articulate these feelings to John, but he refuses to acknowledge her opinion. She finds herself getting angrier with him now, especially when he tells her to exercise self-control.

In particular, the narrator is upset about John's choice of bedroom for her. The narrator prefers a lovely room downstairs that has nice decorations and a window overlooking the garden. However, John argues that the room is too small because it cannot fit two separate beds. He selects instead the nursery room (as indicated by the bars on the windows for children). A big room, the nursery has windows on all sides and allows plenty of sunshine. However, the wallpaper in the room - stripped off in two places - has a hideous, chaotic, yellow pattern, and the narrator can barely stand to look at it. John then enters the room and the narrator puts away her journal, as he hates for her to write.

Analysis

In 1887, Charlotte Perkins Gilman, suffering for several years from depression and fatigue went to see noted physician Silas Weir Mitchell. Mitchell diagnosed her with "neurasthenia" and prescribed the "rest cure" evident in the story. Unable to write or see company, Gilman's rest drove her to the brink of insanity over the next three months. She finally discarded his advice, moved to California, and resumed her work of writing. She soon felt better, and wrote "The Yellow Wallpaper," an exaggerated version of her own experiences. Though Mitchell did not respond when she sent him a copy, she learned later that he had altered his treatment of neurasthenia after reading the story.

Gilman wrote the story not merely to change one man's view of neurasthenia, but to use the story as a symbol of the oppression of women in a paternalistic society. To begin with, we know the name of the narrator's husband (John), but not her own. She is nearly anonymous; her identity is John's wife. This power imbalance extends to other areas of their relationship. John dominates her, albeit in an ultimately patronizing manner. His strong, practical, and stereotypically masculine nature is skeptical of her seemingly weak, "feminine" disorder (as neurasthenia and other mental illnesses were often categorized), and he, not she, diagnoses her problem and prescribes the cure. When he tells her to exercise self-control over her irritation with him, the effect is ironic; he controls nearly everything about her and even makes her feel ungrateful for not valuing his help enough.

The major function of John's control over her, as with Mitchell's control over Gilman, is his inhibiting her from writing. Though she feels writing would help her recover, as Gilman found, John believes it only saps her strength. He stifles her creativity and intellect and forces her into the domesticated position of a powerless wife. The act of hiding her writing whenever John is around is similar to the way literary women in the 18th-century, and even the late 19th-century (when "The Yellow Wallpaper" was written), had to hide their work from their families; Jane Austen is famous for having written her novels while periodically stowing away the manuscripts in her family's living-room.

The narrator is imprisoned, unable to exercise dominion over her mind, and the structure of the house and its surroundings bears this out: "...there are hedges and walls and gates that lock, and lots of separate little houses for the gardeners and people...I never saw such a garden - large and shady, full of box-bordered paths..." Everything is separated and divided, boxed in, and locked like a prison, much as she is held captive in her room. In fact, the house itself seems designed for men; larger-than-life mansions are typically symbols of masculine aggression and competitiveness, while its being a "hereditary estate" reminds us it was probably passed down to men in the family.

Notably, the narrator wanted the more stereotypically feminine room, one that "opened on the piazza," with "roses all over the window, and such pretty old-fashioned chintz hangings!" Despite the airiness of her shared room with John, the barred windows symbolize her imprisonment. That the room may have been a former nursery is more important; she is forced into a helpless, infantile position with John as her caretaker.

In a motif that will assume more importance later in the story, she finds something strange on a "moonlit evening." Night is typically viewed in literature as an escape from the conscious order of the daytime; at night the subconscious runs wild with dreams. Moreover, the moon frequently symbolizes female intuition and sensitivity. Sunshine dominates the nursery during the day, much as John dominates the narrator during the day as he gives her "a schedule prescription for each hour in the day." Thus, sunshine is associated with ordered, masculine oppression, while the night seems to liberate the narrator in some form.

Sunshine is also equated with the yellow wallpaper, which is "faded by the slow-turning sunlight." The "sickly sulphur tint" of wallpaper is also associated with illness. The title of the story clearly indicates that the wallpaper will grow more important, and Gilman hints that the chaos of the wallpaper's pattern will have something to do with the story. For now, we can assume that the chaos has some association with the narrator's seemingly disordered mind. So far she is quite sane, but her narrative style of short sentences that move from topic to topic is similar to the wallpaper's pattern of curves that "plunge off at outrageous angles, destroy themselves in unheard of contradictions." Note, too, that the wallpaper has been stripped off in two parts of the room, a fact that suggests an internal struggle or conflict: perhaps something is trying to break free.

Summary and Analysis of Part 2

It has been two weeks since the narrator and John have moved into the house, and she has not felt like writing since the first day. John is away during the day on cases, even at night sometimes, and the narrator is extremely lonely. She blames John for not understanding how much she suffers and longs for his support. Still, she believes that she is suffering from nothing more than mere nervousness, and she does not want to be a burden to John.

She is too tired to do anything on her own and feels an overwhelming sense of guilt for her incapacity as John's wife. She acknowledges that she is much too nervous to take care of their baby, and she is grateful that their nanny, Mary, is able to take her place.

The wallpaper now irritates the narrator even more since her first day in the house. She attempts to convince John to change the wallpaper, but John laughs at her anxiety. He argues that if they repaper the room for their three-month stay, soon she will want to change everything else in the room, too (which she privately admits is true). Still, the narrator is upset that John dismisses her request so quickly and wishes that there was some way to get rid of the paper.

To avoid looking at the wallpaper, she looks at the garden out of one window, and out of another at the bay, the estate's private wharf, and the shaded lane from the house. She thinks she sees people walking down the lane, but John tells her not to give in to these fanciful visions, as it will exacerbate her nervous condition. The narrator is still convinced that writing would heal her, but she gets tired whenever she tries. John also continues to deny her other hope for her own recovery; he will allow her to see her friends and relatives only after she is well again.

The narrator begins to be preoccupied with the pattern of the wallpaper. She is drawn to a recurrent pattern that looks like a broken neck and two upside-down eyes staring at her. The narrator is also beginning to discern something else in the unruly pattern of the wallpaper: a "strange" figure skulking in the background.

Through the window she sees John's sister, Jennie, a caring and perfect housekeeper, approaching the house. The narrator knows that Jennie spies on her and reports to John so she must make sure not to let her see her writing. The narrator also acknowledges that Jennie probably agrees with John on her diagnosis and believes that the writing has made her sick. As soon as the she hears Jennie coming up the stairs, the narrator puts away her writing and assumes a "restful" position.

Analysis

This section of the story is the first time that the narrator reveals her personal insecurities about her illness. Because of her ailment, the narrator is unable to fulfill her wifely and maternal duties, and she feels that she must be a terrible burden to John. Mary (likely an allusion to the ideal mother: the Virgin Mary) has replaced her as the caretaker of the couple's baby, while Jennie is a model of the perfectly submissive and happily domesticated wife who cares for John's house and welfare.

With the narrator's identities as wife and mother subverted, John acts more like a father to her than he does as a husband. He continues to infantilize her, calling her his "'blessed little goose.'" This paternalistic attitude extends to Jennie, who "hopes for no better profession" than being a housekeeper and who probably believes writing is the cause of the narrator's sickness. Jennie's bias against writing, however, is less forceful than John's is; John stifles the narrator's "imaginative power and habit of story-making" when she merely looks outside and thinks she sees people.

When the narrator attempts to convince him to repaper the nursery, John rejects her request almost immediately. He demonstrates his continued belief in his superiority over the narrator, particularly in terms of her health. By removing the wallpaper, John believes that he will be indulging his patient, submitting to a foolish request. Yet, as the narrator notes, the wallpaper is already extremely damaged, with large spots missing. With that in mind, it seems as if John is refusing the narrator's request simply for the sake of refusing it. He believes that acknowledging her dislike of the wallpaper is ultimately irrational, and he cannot allow himself to perpetuate her nervousness.

John's behavior in this section continues the paternalistic sense of his character that Gilman introduces in the first part of the story. Not only is John oppressively paternalistic as a husband, he is worse because of his position of authority as the narrator's physician. Significantly, John's insistence on keeping the yellow wallpaper in the nursery will ultimately be far more detrimental to the narrator's mental health.

At this point in the story, the narrator also begins to demonstrate some mental issues. Her mind is growing more chaotic and disoriented, mirroring the image of the garden, with its "riotous old-fashioned flowers, and bushes and gnarly trees." This initial chaos is also reflected in her writing, which becomes choppier and more distracted.

The wallpaper is also beginning to take a key position in her mind and daily reality. Instead of focusing on the general hideousness of the wallpaper as she had earlier, now the narrator begins to be preoccupied by specific elements of the pattern. In particular, she is drawn to a central pattern of broken heads and bulbous eyes. This aspect of the pattern is significant in terms of its violence; the popping eyes and deformed neck clearly suggest strangulation or suffocation, both of which relate to the narrator's state of oppression in John's house.

The narrator is also beginning to feels as if the wallpaper is watching her. Not only do John and Jennie watch her, carefully judging and quantifying her behavior, the wallpaper is observing her as well. This adds to the sense of imprisoned surveillance: even when the narrator is alone in the nursery, she is still being monitored. She also claims that she can see a figure in the wallpaper "where the sun is just so." This discovery relates to the sunlight motif and also foreshadows later events in the narrative.

Summary and Analysis of Part 3

The narrator and John have just had relatives over for the 4th of July. Even though Jennie took care of everything, the narrator is still tired and does not know why her health is still failing. John has warned her he may send her to the physician Weir Mitchell in the fall if she does not get better. The narrator is terrified of the prospect of being sent to Weir Mitchell because she has heard that he is the same as John, only more so.

The narrator finds she is anxious, argumentative, and cries easily when alone. John is rarely present, and she begins to feel overwhelmed with her nervousness. She writes only to relieve her thoughts, but the effort is too great even for that. Though she still believes that the key to her recovery lies in writing, she worries that the key to her cure is now beyond her reach.

The narrator attempts to convince John to let her visit Cousin Henry and Julia, but her tears undermine her argument. John carries her back into the nursery and reads to her until she calms down. He then encourages her to use her will power to get better. The narrator's only comfort is that the baby has been well and has not been forced to use the nursery. She is content to know that her presence in the nursery ensures that her baby will not have to suffer the same fate.

With each passing day, the wallpaper proves to be increasingly stimulating. She spends hours studying the confusing, chaotic patterns and even admits that she is beginning to grow rather fond of the wallpaper. Whenever John dismisses her concerns or leaves the house, she immediately finds comfort in the swirling shapes of the yellow wallpaper.

In one sunlit section of the room, she is beginning to make out a more ordered sub-pattern beneath the outer layer, similar to the bars of a cage. The hazy shape beneath the pattern also begins to solidify, and she can now identify it as a woman who is "stooping down and creeping" behind the main pattern.

Analysis

The meaning of the wallpaper is, as the narrator says, growing clearer each day. Beneath the confusing patterns, which closely mirror the narrator's chaotic mind, she image of a woman in a somewhat subservient pose ("stooping down and creeping around"). The figure's position corresponds to the narrator's inferior position in her marriage and in the society.

The bars that appear in the wallpaper continue to emphasize this connection between the narrator and the hazy feminine figure in trapped behind the pattern. Early in the story, the narrator notes the bars on the windows of the nursery, presumably to protect the children from falling out of the windows. Yet, the woman behind the wallpaper is imprisoned behind bars as well, revealing that the narrator is also supposed to be imprisoned in the same way. Perhaps the bars did not even belong to the nursery but were installed in preparation for the narrator's visit.

Significantly, the narrator's perspective toward the wallpaper also begins to change. She is obsessed with the swirling pattern in the wallpaper and even finds comfort in its irrationality when she is sad or lonely. She says: "There are things in that paper that nobody knows but me." Calling it "paper" rather than "wallpaper" suggests that the wallpaper functions similarly to the paper on which she has been secretly writing. The wallpaper is becoming a kind of literary text in which she can discover deep meaning under the surface and develop her own creativity.

Throughout this section, John's paternalism grows. He treats her more like his infant, calling her "his darling and his comfort," as if her identity exists only through him. The narrator also believes "I must take care of myself for his sake," a statement loaded with irony. The irony of John's control over her again resurfaces when he tells her she must use her "will and self-control" to get better when, in fact, he has been controlling her all along.

The narrator's desire to visit her Cousin Henry and Julia is undermined by John's control over her. Although she attempts to outline a clear argument for the visit, John's inability to comprehend her feelings results in a complete emotional breakdown. Because John does not allow the narrator to assume the role of a mature individual in charge of her own life, she is doomed to failure every time she attempts to make a point against him.

Gilman also takes the opportunity to make a boldly insulting reference to S. Weir Mitchell in this section. As the doctor who prescribed Gilman with a similar "rest cure" in 1887, Weir Mitchell is automatically presented as the underlying villain of the story, a physician who is "just like John and my brother, only more so!" The narrator fears Weir Mitchell to such an extent that she would rather stay in the nursery and attempt to cure herself with the wallpaper than see him. John's use of a threat as a way to force the narrator into recovery is also significant, demonstrating his lack of respect for the narrator.

Summary and Analysis of Part 4

One night, the narrator decides that she should talk about her case with John. She hopes to convince him to let them leave the nursery; despite her preoccupation with the wallpaper, she still feels something ominous about it. Yet, the narrator feels insecure talking about her case because she does not want him to think that she doubts him or loves him any less.

Rather than wake him, the narrator gets out of bed to look at the female figure in the wall. When she comes back, John is awake. She asks him if they can leave, but he says their lease is up in three weeks and their house is still being remodeled; besides, she looks like she is getting better. She responds with "Better in body perhaps," but John interrupts and urges her not to think about such things. He goes to sleep, but the narrator stays up for hours staring at the wallpaper.

The wallpaper's pattern continues to absorb the narrator. She is appalled at the irritating pattern and still cannot understand how the pattern can be so torturous. She notices that when the first ray of sunlight shoots through the east window, the pattern changes quickly. By moonlight, the pattern looks completely different. The pattern becomes bars, and the figure of a woman becomes very clear.

As the days pass, John makes the narrator lie down more often for her health. The narrator pretends to follow his orders, but she is unable to sleep and simply follows the pattern of the wallpaper with her eyes. However, she does not want to tell John that she stays awake, and she feels that this is cultivating deceit in their relationship.

The narrator notices that John and Jennie are beginning to act strangely; she is even beginning to be a little afraid of John. Her only explanation for this change in behavior is that they are also interested in the wallpaper. The narrator catches Jennie touching the wallpaper under the excuse that the paper stains clothing. The narrator resolves that no one shall figure out the pattern but her.

Analysis

Gilman continues to develop the motif of sunlight and moonlight as the meaning of wallpaper becomes clearer. By moonlight, the narrator gains the strength to ask John to let her leave the house. Although her plea is unsuccessful, she does not burst into tears as she had during her previous attempt. John ends the discussion by asking the narrator if she trusts him. Significantly, the narrator does not respond and simply pretends to fall asleep.

The pattern of the wallpaper also emerges most clearly by the light of the moon. The narrator is able to identify the figure as a woman behind bars, an image that symbolizes the oppression of female domestication. Because wallpaper is stereotypically a floral, feminine fixture in rooms, the figure's imprisonment behind the wallpaper highlights the expectations for women of the late 19th-century. Unlike men, women of the time were expected only to tend to the housework and the family - and rarely to leave freely for work as John does. The fact that the oppressive wallpaper is on the walls of the nursery is yet another symbol of the maternal duties that the female figure is expected to assume.

However, the narrator only grows subconsciously aware of this oppression at night, when the subconscious is allowed to roam. In the daytime, the figure in the wallpaper is just as repressed as she is: "By daylight she is subdued, quiet. I fancy it is the pattern that keeps her so still."

John continues his condescending, infantilizing behavior toward his "little girl." He asserts that his authority as a physician should be enough to convince her that she is improving; if he says so, it must be true. His refusal to discuss her intimations that she is mentally ill portends disaster.

Yet, the narrator alludes to the possibility that John actually does notice her transformation. She ascribes his strange behavior to an interest in the wallpaper, but it is more likely that John is noticing the narrator's slow loss of rationality. With that in mind, John's indulgent behavior may simply be an attempt to calm the narrator and avoid any major conflicts. His reference to a "little trip of a few days" is particularly pertinent. It is impossible to know if John is actually planning a short trip for the couple or if he is preparing the narrator for a visit with S. Weir Mitchell.

The narrator's prose style grows choppier and more paranoid. She fears that everyone else is trying to figure out the meaning of the wallpaper, particularly Jennie. When she comes upon Jennie touching the wallpaper, the narrator is overcome with rage and has to restrain herself in order not to frighten Jennie. Her final declaration demonstrates the extent of her obsession with the wallpaper: "nobody shall find it out but myself!"

Summary and Analysis of Part 5

The narrator finds life more exciting now because of the wallpaper. Her health improves, and she is calmer, all because of the stimulation provided by the wallpaper; finally she has something to look forward to. Still, she does not tell John that her improving health is due to the wallpaper for fear he would laugh or take her away. She does not want to leave until she has "found it out," and thinks that the remaining week of their vacation will be enough to do so.

Amazed at how much better she feels, the narrator spends most of the daytime sleeping so that she can watch the developments in the wallpaper by night. Every day, new patterns appear in the wallpaper, and the narrator can barely keep track of them. She begins to notice that the wallpaper has its own smell -- a subtle but enduring odor -- that creeps over the entire house and gets in her hair. The "yellow smell" was initially disturbing, but now she is used to it. The narrator also discovers a mark low down on the wall that streaks around the entire room as if it had been rubbed in repeatedly. She wonders why it is there and who did it.

Finally, the narrator has discovered why the wallpaper seems to shake at night: the woman in the wallpaper seizes the bars of the pattern and shakes them as she tries to climb through. Then narrator is not sure if it is only one woman in the wallpaper's pattern crawling around fast, or if there are many women. In the bright spots she is still, and in the darker spots, she shakes the bars of the pattern and tries to climb through. But no one can get through the pattern, which has strangled so many women's heads.

The narrator believes she sees the wallpaper woman outside in the daylight and hiding when others come. She is certain that it is the same woman from behind the wallpaper because of the "creeping," something that most women would never do in daylight. The narrator acknowledges that it must be extremely humiliating to be caught creeping in the daylight; she only creeps during the day when the door is locked and John is gone.

The narrator has only two days left to remove the "top pattern" of the wallpaper off "from the other one." She determines to try and do it, little by little. John and Jennie are growing suspicious of her, and the narrator hears John asking Jennie a series of professional questions about her. Although the narrator is disconcerted by John's strange behavior, she decides that anyone would start to act oddly after sleeping under the yellow wallpaper for three months.

Analysis

The narrator insists that there is something to be "found...out" in the wallpaper. She reinforces the idea of the wallpaper as holding a tangible meaning she can unlock, and Gilman may as well be telling the reader to do the same with "The Yellow

Wallpaper." Both the narrator and the reader try to "peel off" the top pattern of the wallpaper and the story, respectively, to uncover the deeper meaning below.

It is becoming clearer that the woman in the wallpaper represents feminine imprisonment. In her domesticated prison of the wallpaper, she stays subdued and still in bright spots but shakes the "bars" in darker spots. In another allusion to the sunlight/moonlight motif, Gilman associates brightness with the rigidity and regularity of male oppression, and darkness with feminine liberation.

The diffusion of the wallpaper's smell throughout the house symbolizes how the wallpaper is infecting the narrator's mind. She is unable to quantify the odor as anything other than a "yellow smell"; even her powers of observation and imagination have transformed to revolve around the yellow wallpaper. In previous sections, the narrator has been defined entirely by John: as his wife, patient, and property. Here, Gilman suggests that John has been replaced, and the yellow wallpaper now wholly defines the narrator.

As her narrative delivery grows more chaotic and staccato, the narrator identifies more strongly with the woman in the wallpaper. Confusingly, when discussing the woman's habit of "creeping" about outside, the narrator says, "I always lock the door when I creep by daylight." She speaks as if she, and not the woman, is the one doing the creeping.

The narrator is also growing increasingly paranoid and suspicious about John and Jennie. She does not like the way that John is looking at her, and she resents his authoritative questions to Jennie about her. She no longer believes that he is actually loving and kind; instead, she concludes that he is only "pretending" to be loving and kind in an effort to manipulate her. Still, the narrator argues that John cannot be held responsible for his behavior. The influence of the yellow wallpaper has transformed both Jennie and John, and the narrator pities their preoccupation with it.

Clearly, the narrator's sense of reality has become completely warped. No longer recognizing herself as ill, she decides that John and Jennie are the ones being adversely affected by the wallpaper. Moreover, she marks her own behavior as normal by declaring that she only has an "interest" in the wallpaper, nothing more. The narrator seizes control of the situation by placing herself in an authoritative position, capable of judging Jennie and John for herself.

The strange mark around the bottom of the wall foreshadows an action the narrator will take at the end of the story. At this point, the narrator is still unable to recognize it for what it is, a fact that again points to her increasing loss of sanity.

Summary and Analysis of Part 6

They are leaving the house soon, and servants pack up the furniture. John has to stay overnight in town, and the narrator realizes that this is her last chance to free the woman in the wallpaper. Jennie wants to sleep with the narrator, but the narrator tells her that she will sleep better on her own. When the moon comes out, however, the woman in the wallpaper shakes the pattern. The narrator helps her by pulling off the paper. By morning, she has peeled off a head-high strip halfway around the room.

In the morning, Jennie is shocked when she sees the half-stripped wallpaper. The narrator explains that she simply pulled it off because the pattern is so ugly, and Jennie, much relieved, jokes that she would not mind doing it herself. The narrator is suspicious of Jennie and wants to make sure that Jennie does not touch the wallpaper. The narrator "rests" in the nursery and promises to call for Jennie when she wakes up.

Night comes, and the narrator is alone. She locks the door to the nursery and throws the key down into the front path. She wants to astonish John by capturing the woman in the wallpaper and proving that her delusions are real. She has a rope to tie up the woman in case she tries to get away. The narrator continues to strip off the wallpaper, but she cannot reach high up along the wall, and she cannot move the bed to help her. She pulls off what she can reach, and hears within the pattern the "strangled heads and bulbous eyes and fungus growths...shriek with derision."

Frustrated and angry, the narrator wants to jump out the window, but the bars are solid, and she realizes that an action like that might be "misconstrued." Besides, she is afraid to go outside or even look out the window because of all of the women who are creeping about. She wonders if they came out of the wallpaper as she did. She ties herself up with the rope. Though she enjoys creeping about the room, she thinks she will have to get back inside the wallpaper when it "comes night."

John comes home and tries to open the locked door. The narrator tells him where the key is, and he finds it and enters. He asks her what she is doing as she creeps around. She tells him that she has finally gotten out of the wallpaper despite him and Jennie, and that she has pulled off most of the wallpaper so they cannot put her back. John faints, and the narrator keeps creeping over him as she goes around the room.

Analysis

The narrator's insanity climaxes as she identifies completely with the woman in the wallpaper. She believes that not only has the woman come out of the wallpaper, but so has she. Again, the symbolic meaning is that both she and the woman have liberated themselves from masculine oppression; by tearing out of the domesticated prison of the wallpaper, they are free. This moment of liberation again occurs by moonlight when, according to the motif Gilman has drawn, women enjoy a break from the oppression of masculine sunshine.

With her statement that she has gotten out of the wallpaper despite John and Jennie, she suggests that not only her husband, but also the representation of ideal domesticity (in the form of Jennie) has contributed to her imprisonment. She has allowed John and social expectations to dominate her and curb her freedom, but this new self - one made up of the woman in the wallpaper and all the other women she sees "creeping" about - has broken free.

With this in mind, however, the verb "creeping" is an odd choice for this act of breaking free. Creeping - either crawling or walking while hunched over - implies a gesture of subservience. The narrator (and the women creeping outside) is always afraid of being caught, so she must creep about. This may indicate that early feminism needed to "creep" about secretly before it could be respected and acknowledged by the rest of society. The multitudes of women that the narrator sees are perhaps these early practitioners of feminism, who draw strength in their numbers and who, having crept out of the wallpaper, now creep outside.

The narrator's use of the term "work" is also significant in this context. She approaches the destruction of the wallpaper as "work," a job that must be done, yet this in itself is contrary to the expectations of society. The narrator brings a strictly masculine activity into the realm of the domestic sphere and uses it to destroy the oppressive wallpaper. With that in mind, Gilman suggests that the way for women to overcome the oppression of a paternalistic society is to assume the roles of men in the public sphere.

Gilman also drops clues in this section to suggest that the nursery may have been previously used to house the insane. The narrator's total insanity, of course, makes this more evident. The bars on the window are to prevent someone from jumping out, as the narrator contemplates doing; the immovable bed is "fairly gnawed" (and the narrator bites it, too); and the strange mark around the periphery of the room may be from someone else's act of crawling about.

There is one final irony that avenges the narrator's insanity: John's fainting is a stereotypically feminine show of weakness. The narrator finally achieves an authoritative position in her marriage, with John unconscious and her creative imagination finally free of all restraints. Her continual "creeping" over his prone body serves as a repeated emphasis of this liberation, almost as if the narrator chooses to climb over him to highlight his inferiority over and over again.

Suggested Essay Questions

1. How would "The Yellow Wallpaper" be different if it were told from John's point of view?

   If the story were told from John's perspective, it would be a much more detached view of the narrator's descent into madness. Although the readers do not know what John thinks, it is clear that he believes that the medical treatment is correct. Not only would his perspective add another dimension to the woman's madness, but it would make him a more sympathetic character and perhaps even make their love story more tragic.

2. Who does Gilman ultimately blame for the narrator's descent into madness? Why?

   In some ways, Gilman can seem to blame both John and S. Weir Mitchell for the narrator's ultimate insanity. Although they both mean well, their decision to promote the "rest cure" treatment is certainly the catalyst for the narrator's mental break. However, at the same time, Gilman could blame the society of the time, a society that expected women to be perfect wives and mothers and nothing else.

3. What is the significance of the first-person perspective of the narrative?

   The first-person perspective of the narrative is very important because it allows the reader to understand and experience the narrator's descent into madness on a personal level. Instead of discovering the narrator's insanity from the detached perspective of a third-person narrator, the reader is present in the narrator's head at every stage of her insanity. As a result, the story is much more powerful and ultimately more disconcerting.

4. Is John the villain in the story? Why or why not?

   Many literary scholars have argued that John is the clear villain of "The Yellow Wallpaper." Not only does he confine the narrator to the nursery for the "rest cure" treatment, he will not allow her to express her creativity or have any say in her life. However, at the same time, it is apparent that John loves his wife very much and truly wants her to be happy and healthy again. An argument can be made for either side, but the fact remains that John is simply a product of his chauvinistic society.

5. What is the significance of the other female characters in the story?

   The only other female characters who play any sort of role in the story are Mary and Jennie. As the nanny, Mary is immediately presented as an ideal mother figure. This is emphasized by her name, which evokes the image of the Virgin Mary, a stereotype of ideal motherhood. As the house keeper and John's sister, Jennie fulfills all of the other wifely duties neglected by the narrator. Because of her illness (and perhaps because of her propensity to write), the narrator is unable and unwilling to fulfill her socially-accepted duties as a wife and mother.

6. What are some additional meanings behind the color of the wallpaper? How do these explanations change an understanding of the narrative?

One additional reading of the color of the wallpaper is that it promotes a counter-intuitive reading. The color yellow is normally associated with happiness and light; in this case, it is linked to a malignant source that drives the narrator insane. Because the reader expects the color yellow to be benevolent and is disappointed, the reader is also forced to question everything else in the novel, especially those things that seem to be obvious. Other possible readings are that the color of the wallpaper relates to illness (specifically, jaundice) or even that it relates to discriminated minorities of the time period (such as the Chinese).

7. How does "The Yellow Wallpaper" present the conflict between creativity and rationality?

The yellow wallpaper itself is presented as a symbol of creativity. With its endless swirls and ornaments, the wallpaper does not follow any set pattern; in fact, it is this lack of organization and structure that preoccupies the narrator to such an extent. In contrast to the unwieldy creativity of the wallpaper, the majority of the narrator's life is centered in the world of rationality. John, in particular, is devoted to all things rational and criticizes his wife's vivid imagination and penchant for fiction. The narrator is caught in the conflict between these two worlds; her attempt to suppress her creative spirit in favor of John's rationality leads to her mental breakdown.

8. Does "The Yellow Wallpaper" have a happy or sad ending? Explain your answer.

The story ends with the narrator entrenched in complete insanity, certainly not a typical happy ending. Moreover, it is clear to the reader that the marriage is over, and John has finally lost the woman that he loves. However, the ending can also be read as a triumph for the narrator. She has finally freed herself from the constraints of her oppressive society and can revel in the liberty of her creativity. Unfortunately, this liberation goes hand in hand with the loss of her sanity.

9. Would the narrator still have gone insane if she had been confined to a room other than the nursery? Why or why not?

At the beginning of the story, it is unclear if the narrator is actually insane. If she is truly ill, then it is likely that she would have gone mad even if she had not been confined to the nursery. If the narrator is not ill at the start of the story, then the mere confinement and inactivity could have been sufficient to cause a mental breakdown. Either way, the yellow wallpaper serves as an obvious catalyst for her mental deterioration, but we do not know if it is merely a symptom of her insanity or the cause.

10. What happens to the narrator after the story ends?

After the story ends and John returns to consciousness, the narrator would certainly be taken to an insane asylum or sanatorium of some kind. It is possible that John would take her to receive treatment from S. Weir Mitchell, unless the narrator's case was thought to be incurable. The warped liberty that the narrator achieves for herself at the end of "The Yellow Wallpaper" is only transient. If the woman in the wall is not returned to the bars behind the wallpaper, then it is likely that the narrator would be confined behind bars of her own.

Suggested Essay Questions

The "Nervous" Diseases and Hysteria: Medical Predecessors to Neurasthenia

In the "The Yellow Wallpaper," the narrator is diagnosed with neurasthenia, a disease characterized by so-called "nervous exhaustion" and extreme excitability. The narrator is prescribed S. Weir Mitchell's "rest cure" in an effort to calm her nervous depression and allow her to resume her proper position in the household. Significantly, Gilman's story is not the first time that a relationship between weak nerves and women has been highlighted in medical practice. In fact, the idea of nervousness, particularly among females, has dominated medical theory for centuries.

In the 18th century, this type of illness was categorized as one of the "nervous diseases." Named because of their connection to the nerves, or emotions, the nervous diseases were particularly common among women. Because they were thought to have delicate bodies and sensitive minds, women were thought to be extremely susceptible to any disorder that could affect their emotional state.

These nervous diseases were associated with numerous symptoms, such as pale urine, a visible swelling of the stomach, headaches, fainting, palpitations of the heart, long faintings, wind in the stomach and intestines, frequent sighing, giddiness, watching, convulsive crying, convulsive laughing, despair, and melancholy. In other words, any sort of personal dissatisfaction or depression would presumably be a sign of a nervous disease. Although men could also suffer from the nervous diseases, women remained the primary victims because of their physical and mental inferiority to men.

In the nineteenth century, the idea of "nervous diseases" in women underwent transformation and became categorized as a new disease, called "hysteria." Stemming from the Greek word for "uterus," hysteria was immediately presented as a solely feminine ailment. Any activity of the uterus, specifically menstruation, childbirth, or sexual intercourse, was thought to accentuate a woman's vulnerability to hysteria, in the same way that sensitive nerves and general emotional instability would.

Hysterical fits were recognized first by their barrage of emotional and physical symptoms, ranging from heart palpitations, fits, choking, laughing, fainting, and second, by the quick transition from one symptom to the next. Although some physicians argued that hysteria was directly linked to abnormal sexual activity, the disease was generally understood to result from emotional sensitivity or "nervousness" on a fundamental level.

As a disease, neurasthenia has clear similarities to both the nervous diseases and hysteria and can be recognized as a relative, if not descendant, of the other two. Neurasthenia was first described in 1869 as a disease characterized by depression, extreme anxiety, and fatigue.

When the narrator is diagnosed with neurasthenia, it is significant to note that she also exhibits symptoms of the two other diseases, particularly as the yellow wallpaper begins to affect her. Her fatigue and depression correspond closely to the symptoms of neurasthenia. At the same time, her constant melancholy and mental and emotional agitation are sure signs of the nervous diseases. Finally, hysteria is highlighted in the fact that the narrator is a new mother; her mental instability could certainly be seen as a result of her female physiognomy.

While the narrator eventually shows elements of each of these diseases, it is unclear if the narrator is ill when the story begins. In the first few paragraphs, her only palpable symptoms are mild depression and a desire to express her creativity through writing; she certainly does not seem to be the typical patient for the "rest cure."

Whether or not she is actually ill, the narrator is still immediately forced to accept a diagnosis that insists that her melancholy restlessness is due to weak nerves, emotional incapacity, and her feminine nature. Whether the diagnosis actually corresponds to the symptoms of the nervous diseases, hysteria, or neurasthenia, the fact remains that the narrator is forced to undergo a treatment that suppresses her creativity and emphasizes her inferiority to men. Moreover, as the historical background of these diseases suggests, the medical doctrine of the time was ultimately sexist and oppressive. The narrator is not only at odds with her husband and brother; she is placed in direct conflict with centuries of medical practice and beliefs about female nerves and female reproduction.

Perhaps the narrator is truly an honest victim of the sensitive nerves and active uterus that characterized the nervous diseases and hysteria. Then again, perhaps she is forced to endure the "rest cure" in order to quell her creative inclinations and allow her to take on the role of a proper wife to her husband. Either way, as the narrator plunges deeper into the world of the yellow wallpaper, the reader cannot help but wonder how many other "nervous" or "hysterical" women have suffered the same fate.

Author of ClassicNote and Sources

Teddy Wayne, author of ClassicNote. Completed on September 29, 2002, copyright held by GradeSaver.

Updated and revised Caitlin Vincent November 30, 2008. Copyright held by GradeSaver.

Gilman, Charlotte Perkins. The Yellow Wallpaper and Other Writings. New York: Bantam Dell/ Random House, Inc., 2006.

Barbara Hill Rigney. Madness and Sexual Politics in the Feminist Novel: Studies in Bronte, Woolf, Lessing, and Atwood. Madison: University of Wisconsin Press, 1980.

Susan Bordo, Leslie Heywood. Unbearable Weight: Feminism, Western Culture, and the Body. Berkeley: University of California Press, 2003.

Ann J. Lane. To Herland and Beyond: The Life and Work of Charlotte Perkins Gilman. Charlottesville: University of Virginia Press, 1997.

Catherine Golden, Joanna S. Zangrando. The Mixed Legacy of Charlotte Perkins Gilman. Newark: University of Delaware Press, 2000.

Haney-Peritz, Janice. "Monumental Feminism and Literature's Ancestral House: Another Look at 'The Yellow Wallpaper.'" Women's Studies 12 (1986): 113-128.

Hume, Beverly A. "Gilman's 'Interminable Grotesque': The Narrator of 'The Yellow Wallpaper.'" Studies in Short Fiction 28 (Fall 1991): 477-484.

King, Jeannette, and Pam Morris. "On Not Reading Between the Lines: Models of Reading in 'The Yellow Wallpaper.'" Studies in Short Fiction 26.1 (Winter 1989): 23-32.

Lanser, Susan S. "Feminist Criticism, 'The Yellow Wallpaper,' and the Politics of Color in America." Feminist Studies 15 (Fall 1989): 415-437.

Oakley, Ann. "Beyond the Yellow Wallpaper." Reproductive Health Matters, Vol. 5, No. 10 (November 1997): 29-39.

Ford, Karen. "'The Yellow Wallpaper' and Women's Discourse." Tulsa Studies in Women's Literature, Vol. 4, No. 2 (Autumn 1985): 309-314.

Treichler, Paula A. "Escaping the Sentence: Diagnosis and Discourse in 'The Yellow Wallpaper.'" Tulsa Studies in Women's Literature, Vol. 3, No. 1/2 (Autumn 1984):

61-77.

Shumaker, Conrad. "'To Terribly Good to Be Printed': Charlotte Gilman's 'The Yellow Wallpaper.'" American Literature, Vol. 57, No. 4 (December 1985): 588-599.

St. Jean, Shawn. "Hanging 'The Yellow Wall-Paper': Feminisim and Textual Studies." Feminist Studies, Vol. 28, No. 2 (Summer 2002): 397-415.

Dock, Julie Bates. "'But One Expects That': Charlotte Perkins Gilman's 'The Yellow Wallpaper' and the Shifting Light of Scholarship." PMLA, Vol. 111, No. 1 (January 1996): 52-65.

Essay: Responding to the Wallpaper

by Rebecca Edwards
June 29, 2002

> "The pattern is torturing. You think you have mastered it, but just as you get well underway in following, it turns a back-somersault and there you are. It slaps you in the face, knocks you down, and tramples upon you."

As her madness progresses the narrator in The Yellow Wallpaper becomes increasingly aware of a woman present in the pattern of the wallpaper. She sees this woman struggling against the paper's "bars". Later in her madness she imagines there to be many women lost in its "torturing" pattern, trying in vain to climb through it. The woman caught in the wallpaper seems to parallel the narrator's virtual imprisonment by her well-meaning husband. While the narrator's perception of the wallpaper reveals her increasing madness, it effectively symbolizes the struggle of women who attempt to break out of society's feminine standards.

The narrator writes furtively in her room, having to hide her writing from her family. They feel that her only road to recovery is through total R & R, that she should not have to lift a finger, let alone stimulate a single neuron in her female brain. While she appreciates their concern she feels stifled and bored. She feels that her condition is only being worsened by her lack of stimulus, but it is not simply boredom that bothers her. She is constantly feeling guilty and unappreciative for questioning her family's advice. This causes her to question her self-awareness and her own perception of reality. "I sometimes fancy that in my condition if I had less opposition and more society and stimulus; but John says the very worst thing I can do is to think about my condition, and I confess it always makes me feel bad." She also faults herself for not taking care of her home and family. Like Dickinson, she is caught up in the cobwebs of her society's ideology.

She has an immediate dislike for the wallpaper and at first studies it with the eye of a critical interior decorator. The pattern fascinates her and she becomes increasingly obsessed with uncovering its secrets. Eventually it becomes the center of her life and her only concern. On the most basic level, it is apparent that anyone who becomes obsessed with wallpaper and believes it to hold a world that people inhabit is insane. Looking deeper into what the narrator reads into the wallpaper, we can understand her more clearly. The woman she sees in the wallpaper struggling to break free of the bars seems to reflect and reinforce her own desire to leave the house. When she first writes of the woman shaking the wallpaper at night, trying to escape, this coincides with her attempt to convince her husband to take her away from the place. Neither woman is successful in breaking away and the narrator begins to read even more into the pattern. While outwardly and on a conscious level she accepts John's refusal to leave, she seems to be projecting her real anger and resentment onto the wallpaper;

The pattern "slaps you in the face, knocks you down, and tramples upon you."

After this incident, and following description of the "torturing" pattern, she begins to be protective of the wallpaper. She becomes paranoid of anyone infringing on her territory; "I know she was studying that pattern, and I am determined that no one shall find it out but myself!" It has become personal to her, a place where she sees her own feelings projected. As she tries to understand the pattern, it is as if she is trying to understand herself and how her own mind is working. As she becomes more and more withdrawn, she becomes more fixated on the wallpaper. As her mental state unravels, she sees more and more frenzied activity in the wallpaper, and eventually feels the need to physically pull the wallpaper off the wall. With this final act she seems to lose what little sense she has left, and the story ends with her crawling around on the floor like an animal.

While the wallpaper provides a haven for the narrator, and the activity on it reflects her mental state, there seems to be a deeper meaning in it. As the narrator goes progressively more insane, she actually becomes much calmer in her writing. The tone becomes less anxious, more analytical, and suggests that she is finding some rational meaning in the pattern on the wall. As she tries to stimulate her mind and break out of the role of being the docile wife she runs up against the wall of society and their resistance to bending of gender roles. As a woman, it is not even conceivable that it is her mind that needs to be treated, so even as she sees what is wrong with her and desires some mental stimulation, she is told nicely to shut up and go to bed. While at the beginning she is simply depressed, she is driven mad by the restraints society places on her. The women she sees in the wallpaper are trying desperately to break through the pattern on the wall that restrains them, just as society does. As hard as they try they can't get figure out how to break out; "You think you have mastered it, but just as you get well underway in following, it turns a back somersault and there you are."

The pattern of the yellow wallpaper reflects the mental state of the narrator, as she projects her feelings onto it. The pattern also represents the limits society places on women and the resistance of society to women, such as her, who are trying to break free.

Essay: The Stages of Feminine Injustice

by Tara Rudrapatna
November 03, 2004

In the well-known work Women and Economics, Charlotte Perkins Gilman emphasizes her belief that "dependence on men not only doom[s] women to live stifled lives but also retard[s] the development of the human species" (Kirszner 449). Those words support the ideas conveyed in her short story, "A Yellow Wallpaper". In this piece, the narrator undergoes three stages: first, she develops a mental illness resulting from the constrictions of a male-dominated society; second, she deteriorates due to a worsening environment; and finally, she reaches a state of insanity. Ironically, it is this final stage that symbolizes her freedom.

In the beginning, Gilman reveals how the confinements of a restrictive society induce the narrator's illness. In the opening lines, she immediately points out the imbalance in her marriage: "there is something queer about [this house]...John laughs at me, of course, but one expects that in marriage" (Gilman 450). The narrator implicitly accepts that her opinions are "frivolous", trying to justify her sense that her thoughts are not worthy of her husband's respect. She goes on to demonstrate her husband's dominance in their relationship: "There comes John, and I must put this away - he hates to have me write a word" (451). His domination and her implicit submission emphasize the confinement of her environment. In these two distinct areas, Gilman offers two key assumptions about a patriarchal society: the value of the male mind over the "seemingly weak and foolish" mindset of the female, and the derivation of power in males, who direct the lives of females.

Gilman also stresses the nature of female docility and its strong presence within the conventions of society. Furthermore, her illness originates in her restrictive environment. Critic Ann Lane writes that "imaginative women who found themselves with no outlets for their abilities, while in the larger culture opportunities proliferated for ambitious and imaginative men, suffered particularly" (467). Lane's analysis implies that the narrator's restricted writing and her disregard for her own concerns are the primary causes for her illness. In this first phase, Gilman illustrates the detrimental effects that male dominance can have on female health.

The narrator's stifling environment furthers the progress of her debilitating disease. In the first stage, we see how harmful she finds her confining surroundings. It is logical to assume that continued confinement will only harm her further. However, John fails to follow this logic. The narrator repeatedly tries to convey her concerns, but is continually discouraged: "At first he meant to repaper the room, but afterwards he said that I was letting it get the better of me, and that nothing was worse for a nervous patient than to give way to such fancies...Then he took me in his arms and called me a blessed little goose" (Gilman 452). The husband discourages the narrator from letting the wallpaper "get the better of her" - instead of trying to see deeper into her fears, he only disregards them. He forces his opinions and judgments on her while ignoring her needs. John's disregard is further exemplified by his treatment of the narrator: he calls her a "little goose", implying that her fears are insignificant. However, this does not solve the problem, but only forces the narrator to bottle up her feelings. As Sandra Gilbert and Susan Gubar write, the story is "a paradigmatic tale which seems to tell the story that all literary women would tell if they could speak their 'speechless woe'" (464). Literary women are stifled in much the same way as the narrator, and the anxiety she suffers only makes her situation worse. Later, the narrator admits, "So of course I said no more on that score...and lay there for hours trying to decide whether that front pattern and the back pattern really did move together" (Gilman 456). Bottling up her feelings and thoughts only increases her problems, and her mind grows even more unstable. Gilbert and Gubar affirm this notion, writing that "As time passes, this figure concealed behind what corresponds to the faade of the patriarchal text becomes clearer...the wallpaper 'becomes bars!'...[and] the narrator sinks more deeply into what the world calls madness" (465). In this manner, Gilman demonstrates how the narrator's environment hastens her deterioration.

The eventual breakdown of the narrator's mental state into total insanity allows for her ultimate release. Her insanity replaces the conventions of male domination with a new form of reality. The hallucinations created by the narrator's illness foreshadow a sense of freedom. The woman behind the wallpaper possesses far more freedom than the author: "I have watched her sometimes away off in the open country, creeping as fast as a cloud shadow in a high wind" (Gilman 459). The woman has the freedom to travel outside, "in the open country" - a space with no restrictions. She includes sky imagery such as a "cloud in a high wind", images that are typically associated with freedom. In a perverse way, the narrator glorifies her hallucinations and, more importantly, her very insanity. Gilbert and Gubar concur: "More significant are the madwoman's won imaginings and creations, mirages of health and freedom with which her author endows her like a fairy godmother showering fold on a sleeping heroine" (466). Additionally, the shift in John's behavior at the end of the story, when he faints in response to the narrator's behavior, reveals a role reversal. The male has become weaker and is divested of power, while the female is set free. The narrator even scoffs at her husband's feminine reaction to her power, recalling John's attitude at the beginning of the story. Gilbert and Gubar add, "Doctor John...has been defeated...[in] John's unmasculine swoon of surprise" (465). Gilbert and Gubar see this moment as a defeat not only for John, but for all men. The narrator's insanity not only shows the inefficacy of the "Rest Cure", but demonstrates how the disease can, paradoxically, have a momentous outcome.

The shifts throughout "The Yellow Wallpaper" illustrate the detrimental effects of feminine subordination. Furthermore, they reveal the consequences of male domination, which may in some cases alter the standards of a patriarchal society. In fact, the narrator in Gilman's story accomplishes just this: she is able to effect change in her own society. She has the most success in the case of her former doctor, Silas Weir Mitchell, effectively altering "his treatment of nervous prostration" (Gilbert

466). In response to this, the narrator famously declares, "If that is a fact, then I have not lived in vain" (466).

WORKS CITED

Gilbert, Sandra M., and Susan Gubar. The Madwoman in the Attic: The Woman Writer and the Nineteenth-Century Literary Imagination. Kirszner and Mandell 464-66.

Gilman, Charlotte Perkins. "The Yellow Wallpaper." Kirszner and Mandell 450-61.

Lane, Ann. To Herland and Beyond: The Life and Works of Charlotte Perkins Gilman. Kirszner and Mandell 466-70.

Kirszner, Laurie G., and Stephen R. Mandell. Literature: Reading, Reacting, Writing. 5th ed. Boston: Heinle, 2004.

Quiz 1

1. **What is John's profession?**
   A. Lawyer
   B. Writer
   C. Dentist
   D. Physician

2. **What is the narrator's brother's profession?**
   A. Lawyer
   B. Writer
   C. Dentist
   D. Physician

3. **To what physician does John at one point threaten to send the narrator?**
   A. Weir Mitchell
   B. Horace Scudder
   C. Her father
   D. Her brother

4. **What is the name of the nanny?**
   A. Jennie
   B. Jane
   C. Mary
   D. She does not have one

5. **Who tends to the house?**
   A. Jennie
   B. Jane
   C. John
   D. Mary

6. **What kind of house are they in?**
   A. A small cottage
   B. A colonial mansion
   C. A Victorian mansion
   D. A cabin

7. **What is happening to the couple's own house while they are away?**
    A. It is being remodeled
    B. It is being sold
    C. They have rented it out
    D. It has burned down

8. **What kind of a room does the narrator believe her room once was?**
    A. A nursery
    B. A bathroom
    C. A family room
    D. A living room

9. **What is one major similarity between the narrator's room and the wallpaper's pattern?**
    A. They both are chaotic
    B. They both have windows
    C. They both do not let in sunlight
    D. They both have bars

10. **What is caught in the wallpaper's pattern?**
    A. Trapped hands
    B. Nothing
    C. Strangled heads
    D. Men

11. **What does the woman do at night within the wallpaper?**
    A. She shakes at the bars
    B. She cries
    C. She sleeps
    D. She sits silently

12. **With what diminutive does John frequently refer to the narrator?**
    A. "Petite"
    B. "Little"
    C. "Tiny"
    D. "Small"

13. **Who officially decides what the narrator should do during the day?**
    A. Jennie
    B. John
    C. Mary
    D. The narrator

14. **What does John prevent the narrator from doing most of all?**
    A. Reading
    B. Writing
    C. Walking around
    D. Painting

15. **What word does the narrator frequently use to describe the movement of the woman in the wallpaper?**
    A. "Running"
    B. "Creeping"
    C. "Crawling"
    D. "Stooping"

16. **When is the woman most visible in the wallpaper?**
    A. At noon
    B. In the sunlight
    C. In the afternoon
    D. By moonlight

17. **When does the woman in the wallpaper stop moving?**
    A. At noon
    B. In the sunlight
    C. In the afternoon
    D. By moonlight

18. **When does the narrator usually sleep?**
    A. During the day
    B. At night
    C. At 5 P.M.
    D. At 6 P.M.

19. **What condition is the narrator thought to suffer from?**
    A. Neurasthenia
    B. Hypertension
    C. Seasonal Affective Disorder
    D. Cancer

20. **How does the narrator describe the odor of the wallpaper?**
    A. As a "banana smell"
    B. As a "lemony smell"
    C. As a "yellow smell"
    D. As a "wallpaper-like smell"

21. **What does John do at the end of the story?**
    A. He cries
    B. He faints
    C. He kills himself
    D. He jumps out of the window

22. **The narrator tells John she has gotten out of the wallpaper despite him and who else?**
    A. Jennie
    B. Weir Mitchell
    C. Jane
    D. Mary

23. **Whom does the narrator want to visit although John will not let her?**
    A. Weir Mitchell
    B. Her baby
    C. Relatives
    D. Mary

24. **What is the strange mark around the bottom of the wall probably from?**
    A. A child's prank
    B. The guideline to putting up the wallpaper
    C. Someone else who crawled around the periphery of the room
    D. Measurements of the room

25. **How does John generally treat the narrator?**
    A. As his daughter
    B. As his grandmother
    C. As his mother
    D. As his sister

Quiz 1 Answer Key

1. **(D)** Physician
2. **(D)** Physician
3. **(A)** Weir Mitchell
4. **(C)** Mary
5. **(A)** Jennie
6. **(B)** A colonial mansion
7. **(A)** It is being remodeled
8. **(A)** A nursery
9. **(D)** They both have bars
10. **(C)** Strangled heads
11. **(A)** She shakes at the bars
12. **(B)** "Little"
13. **(B)** John
14. **(B)** Writing
15. **(B)** "Creeping"
16. **(D)** By moonlight
17. **(B)** In the sunlight
18. **(A)** During the day
19. **(A)** Neurasthenia
20. **(C)** As a "yellow smell"
21. **(B)** He faints
22. **(C)** Jane
23. **(C)** Relatives
24. **(C)** Someone else who crawled around the periphery of the room
25. **(A)** As his daughter

Quiz 2

1. **Why does John claim he wants the narrator to use the room she is in?**
    A. Because it is away from the baby
    B. Because it is airy
    C. Because it is on the second floor
    D. Because it is small

2. **Who prescribed Gilman a similar "rest cure" when she suffered from depression?**
    A. William Dean Howells
    B. Her father
    C. Her brother
    D. Silas Weir Mitchell

3. **For how long did Gilman endure the rest cure?**
    A. One day
    B. One week
    C. One year
    D. Three months

4. **What, according to Gilman, rescued her from insanity?**
    A. Writing
    B. Exercise
    C. Painting
    D. Phosphates

5. **Why did Horace Scudder say he rejected "The Yellow Wallpaper" for publication?**
    A. Because it was too feminist
    B. Because it was poorly written
    C. Because his wife suffered from neurasthenia
    D. Because it was depressing

6. **In what year was "The Yellow Wallpaper" published?**
    A. 1776
    B. 1868
    C. 1892
    D. 1920

7. **Who left Gilman and her family when she was a child?**
   A. Gilman's grandmother
   B. Gilman's father
   C. Gilman's mother
   D. Gilman's brother

8. **How did Gilman die?**
   A. breast cancer
   B. suicide
   C. car accident
   D. brain cancer

9. **Where did Gilman move after separating from her first husband?**
   A. London
   B. California
   C. Paris
   D. New York City

10. **Which of the following works did Gilman NOT write?**
    A. "The Yellow Wallpaper"
    B. "A Vindication of the Rights of Woman"
    C. "Herland"
    D. "Women and Economics"

11. **Who was Gilman's famous relative?**
    A. Mary Wollstonecraft
    B. Harriet Beecher Stowe
    C. James Joyce
    D. Ralph Waldo Emerson

12. **Which of the following is NOT one of the ways in which the narrator describes John?**
    A. He has an intense horror of superstition
    B. He has no patience with faith
    C. He is practical to the extreme
    D. He does not believe in God

13. **What does the narrator believe is the biggest problem with John?**
    A. He spends too much time with his patients
    B. He does not believe that she is sick
    C. He will not remove the wallpaper from the nursery
    D. He does not want any more children

14. **When did Gilman marry her first husband?**
    A. 1860
    B. 1884
    C. 1900
    D. 1915

15. **What does John diagnose the narrator with?**
    A. A slight hysterical tendency
    B. Allergies
    C. Post-partum depression
    D. A slight cold

16. **Which treatment does John NOT suggest for the narrator to get well?**
    A. Tonics
    B. Time in society
    C. Fresh air
    D. Phosphates

17. **Why does John reject the room that the narrator prefers?**
    A. The wallpaper is not yellow enough
    B. There is only one window
    C. The chintz hangings aggravate his allergies
    D. The piazza would be a distraction

18. **How does the narrator describe the color of the wallpaper?**
    A. Dull and boring
    B. Charming and cheerful
    C. Bright and happy
    D. Repellent and revolting

19. **What does John call the narrator when she complains about the wallpaper?**
    A. A crazy little thing
    B. A blessed little goose
    C. A sweet little girl
    D. A silly woman

20. **What does John compare a visit from Cousin Henry to?**
    A. Ants at a picnic
    B. Additional swirls in the wallpaper
    C. Too much wine at dinner
    D. Fireworks in a pillow-case

21. **What does the narrator imagine she sees on the shady lane outside of the house?**
    A. People walking
    B. Her baby with Mary
    C. Dogs playing
    D. John having a picnic

22. **What could the name "Mary" possibly signify?**
    A. Mary Wollstonecraft
    B. The Virgin Mary
    C. Mary from "Mary had a little lamb"
    D. Mary, Queen of Scots

23. **What happens when the narrator attempts to write?**
    A. She becomes very tired
    B. She becomes very hungry
    C. She thinks about how much she loves John
    D. She becomes violent

24. **What recurrent image does the narrator see in the wallpaper?**
    A. bulbous eyes
    B. misspelled words
    C. broken legs
    D. twisted hair

25. **What will John threaten to do if the narrrator does not get better?**

    A. Kill her
    B. Send her to her mother's house
    C. Divorce her
    D. Send her to S. Weir Mitchell

Quiz 2 Answer Key

1. **(B)** Because it is airy
2. **(D)** Silas Weir Mitchell
3. **(D)** Three months
4. **(A)** Writing
5. **(D)** Because it was depressing
6. **(C)** 1892
7. **(B)** Gilman's father
8. **(B)** suicide
9. **(B)** California
10. **(B)** "A Vindication of the Rights of Woman"
11. **(B)** Harriet Beecher Stowe
12. **(D)** He does not believe in God
13. **(B)** He does not believe that she is sick
14. **(B)** 1884
15. **(A)** A slight hysterical tendency
16. **(B)** Time in society
17. **(B)** There is only one window
18. **(D)** Repellent and revolting
19. **(B)** A blessed little goose
20. **(D)** Fireworks in a pillow-case
21. **(A)** People walking
22. **(B)** The Virgin Mary
23. **(A)** She becomes very tired
24. **(A)** bulbous eyes
25. **(D)** Send her to S. Weir Mitchell

Quiz 3

1. **What does the narrator describe as being "as good as gymnastics"?**
   A. Playing with the baby
   B. Arguing with John
   C. Running around the house
   D. Following the pattern of the wallpaper

2. **Where did Gilman go to college?**
   A. University of Rhode Island
   B. Rhode Island School of Design
   C. Radcliffe College
   D. Johns Hopkins University

3. **How does the narrator describe the pattern of the wallpaper?**
   A. A nauseating collection of twisted heads and wandering eyes
   B. A hovering wall of snakes and seaweed
   C. A kind of "debased Romanesque" with delirium tremens
   D. A series of spastic swirls

4. **Why does John say the narrator must take care of herself?**
   A. For her mother's sake
   B. For her sake
   C. For his sake
   D. For the sake of their child

5. **What is the narrator's one consolation for staying in the nursery?**
   A. The baby does not have to stay there
   B. Their rent is cheaper
   C. The floors are easier to clean
   D. John does not like the wallpaper either

6. **What does the figure in the wall do?**
   A. Pull on the broken heads and bulbous eyes
   B. Dance in the moonlight
   C. Scratch the narrator while she is sleeping
   D. Shake the bars of the wallpaper

7. **What does the narrator eventually realize about the pattern of the wallpaper?**
    A. There is a front pattern and a back pattern
    B. The pattern is based on geometric principles
    C. There is no pattern
    D. She has drawn the pattern herself

8. **When is the true nature of the wallpaper exposed?**
    A. In the early morning
    B. At dusk
    C. During the afternoon
    D. At night

9. **Which of the following does the pattern of the wallpaper NOT do to an observer?**
    A. Knock you down
    B. Caress you
    C. Trample you
    D. Slap you in the face

10. **What happens to the wallpaper at night?**
    A. It tries to strangle the narrator
    B. It comes alive
    C. It becomes bars
    D. It turns blue

11. **What is the woman in the wallpaper trying to do?**
    A. Climb through
    B. Kill John
    C. Kill the narrator
    D. Write

12. **Why is the woman in the wallpaper unable to escape on her own?**
    A. There are too many shades of yellow
    B. There are too many strangling heads
    C. There are too many bars
    D. There are too many bright spots

13. **Who does the narrator see creeping by daylight?**
    A. John
    B. Mary
    C. Jenny
    D. The woman in the wallpaper

14. **What does the narrator do during her last night in the nursery?**
    A. Strip off all the wallpaper
    B. Sleep
    C. Spend time with John
    D. Swim naked in the bay

15. **What does the narrator do with the key after she locks herself in the nursery?**
    A. Cover it with strips of wallpaper
    B. Throw it outside
    C. Put it in her pocket
    D. Hide it under the bed

16. **Where does the narrator tell John to find the key?**
    A. Next to the pine tree
    B. Under a plantain leaf
    C. Under a maple leaf
    D. Under the doormat

17. **At the end of the story, who does the narrator have to step over when she is creeping?**
    A. John
    B. Mary
    C. Jenny
    D. The woman in the wallpaper

18. **What is the yellow of the wallpaper NOT like?**
    A. Butter
    B. Cheddar cheese
    C. Sunlight
    D. Buttercups

19. **What is the format of the story?**
   A. Dialogue
   B. First-person journal entries
   C. Third-person stream of consciousness
   D. Third-person description

20. **What is the point of view of the narrative?**
   A. Jennie's perspective
   B. John's perspective
   C. Third person
   D. First person

21. **What is odd about the bed in the nursery?**
   A. It is very small
   B. It has teethmarks on it
   C. It smells of death
   D. It is yellow

22. **In what year was Gilman treated by Weir Mitchell?**
   A. 1875
   B. 1887
   C. 1892
   D. 1905

23. **In what year did Gilman die?**
   A. 1892
   B. 1915
   C. 1935
   D. 1945

24. **What was the name of Gilman's first husband?**
   A. S. Weir Mitchell
   B. George Houghton Gilman
   C. Charles Walter Stetson
   D. John Joyce

25. **Which of Gilman's other works describes a utopian society composed solely of women?**
    A. The Yellow Wallpaper
    B. The Home
    C. Herland
    D. Women and Economics

Quiz 3 Answer Key

1. **(D)** Following the pattern of the wallpaper
2. **(B)** Rhode Island School of Design
3. **(C)** A kind of "debased Romanesque" with delirium tremens
4. **(C)** For his sake
5. **(A)** The baby does not have to stay there
6. **(D)** Shake the bars of the wallpaper
7. **(A)** There is a front pattern and a back pattern
8. **(D)** At night
9. **(B)** Caress you
10. **(C)** It becomes bars
11. **(A)** Climb through
12. **(B)** There are too many strangling heads
13. **(D)** The woman in the wallpaper
14. **(A)** Strip off all the wallpaper
15. **(B)** Throw it outside
16. **(B)** Under a plantain leaf
17. **(A)** John
18. **(D)** Buttercups
19. **(B)** First-person journal entries
20. **(D)** First person
21. **(B)** It has teethmarks on it
22. **(B)** 1887
23. **(C)** 1935
24. **(C)** Charles Walter Stetson
25. **(C)** Herland

Quiz 4

1. **Why does the narrator strip off all the wallpaper on her last day in the nursery?**
   A. To punish John
   B. To let the woman out of the wall
   C. To make Jennie clean up the mess
   D. To express her anger at being confined

2. **What could the narrator's "neurasthenia" actually have been?**
   A. Schizophrenia
   B. Post-partum depression
   C. Bi-polar disorder
   D. Narcissism

3. **What is the name of the narrator?**
   A. Jennie
   B. She has no name
   C. Rebecca
   D. Mary

4. **Where did Gilman grow up?**
   A. New York
   B. Massachusetts
   C. Virginia
   D. Rhode Island

5. **How does the narrator refer to John at the end of the story?**
   A. My love
   B. Darling
   C. Husband
   D. That man

6. **How does the narrator describe herself and John at the beginning of the story?**
   A. Nobles
   B. Paupers
   C. Extraordinary people
   D. Ordinary people

7. **What term does the narrator use to describe the house when she first sees it?**
   A. Lovely
   B. Inviting
   C. Odd
   D. Queer

8. **Why do the windows in the nursery have bars on them?**
   A. So that children would not fall out
   B. To add to the ghostliness of the house
   C. For aesthetic purposes
   D. To keep the narrator from committing suicide

9. **Who visited the narrator over the Fourth of July weekend?**
   A. Weir Mitchell
   B. Jennie and Mary
   C. Cousin Henry and Julia
   D. Mother and Nellie

10. **Why does the narrator have a rope?**
    A. To hang herself
    B. To tie up the woman in the wall
    C. To strangle John
    D. To climb out of the window

11. **How does the narrator describe her journal?**
    A. As the wallpaper
    B. As her only friend
    C. As her lover
    D. As dead paper

12. **What is Gilman's middle name?**
    A. Harriet
    B. Anna
    C. Beth
    D. Jane

13. **In what year did Gilman marry her second husband?**
    A. 1884
    B. 1900
    C. 1910
    D. 1930

14. **In what year did Gilman begin to write her autobiography?**
    A. 1892
    B. 1900
    C. 1925
    D. 1935

15. **What was the name of Gilman's daughter?**
    A. Jennie
    B. Katharine
    C. Elizabeth
    D. Charlotte

16. **What was forbidden to a woman undergoing the "rest cure"?**
    A. Fatty foods
    B. Inactivity
    C. Creative activity
    D. Sleep

17. **To whom did Gilman send the first draft of "The Yellow Wallpaper" in 1890?**
    A. William Dean Howells
    B. S. Weir Mitchell
    C. Harriet Beecher Stowe
    D. James Joyce

18. **To whom was Gilman compared when "The Yellow Wallpaper" was first published?**
    A. Fanny Burney and Eliza Heywood
    B. Edgar Allen Poe and Mary Shelley
    C. Jane Austen and Charlotte Bronte
    D. Emily Bronte and Daphne du Maurier

19. **Who is Jennie?**
    A. The narrator's cousin
    B. The narrator's sister
    C. John's cousin
    D. John's sister

20. **What might moonlight symbolize in the story?**
    A. Liberation
    B. Oppression
    C. Domesticity
    D. Unhappiness

21. **Which of the narrator's qualities is the most disconcerting to John?**
    A. Her literary skills
    B. Her imagination
    C. Her beauty
    D. Her stubbornness

22. **How much time passes between the narrator's first two journal entries?**
    A. One day
    B. One week
    C. Four days
    D. Two weeks

23. **Over the course of the story, which of the following does NOT happen to the narrator?**
    A. She becomes more fond of John
    B. She becomes more depressed and cries easily
    C. She becomes tired more quickly
    D. She becomes paranoid that Jennie and John are trying to figure out the meaning of the wallpaper

24. **What does the narrator believe is the cause of her improving physical health?**
    A. The wallpaper
    B. Constant sleep
    C. John's treatment
    D. Fatty foods

25. **Why is John absent during their last night in the nursery?**
    A. He needs a break from the yellow wallpaper
    B. He is on his way to fetch Weir Mitchell
    C. He is disgusted by the narrator's growing insanity
    D. He has to stay overnight in town

Quiz 4 Answer Key

1. **(B)** To let the woman out of the wall
2. **(B)** Post-partum depression
3. **(B)** She has no name
4. **(D)** Rhode Island
5. **(D)** That man
6. **(D)** Ordinary people
7. **(D)** Queer
8. **(A)** So that children would not fall out
9. **(D)** Mother and Nellie
10. **(B)** To tie up the woman in the wall
11. **(D)** As dead paper
12. **(B)** Anna
13. **(B)** 1900
14. **(C)** 1925
15. **(B)** Katharine
16. **(C)** Creative activity
17. **(A)** William Dean Howells
18. **(B)** Edgar Allen Poe and Mary Shelley
19. **(D)** John's sister
20. **(A)** Liberation
21. **(B)** Her imagination
22. **(D)** Two weeks
23. **(A)** She becomes more fond of John
24. **(A)** The wallpaper
25. **(D)** He has to stay overnight in town

ClassicNotes

GradeSaver™

Getting you the grade since 1999™

Other ClassicNotes from GradeSaver™

1984
Absalom, Absalom
Adam Bede
The Adventures of Augie
   March
The Adventures of
   Huckleberry Finn
The Adventures of Tom
   Sawyer
The Aeneid
Agamemnon
The Age of Innocence
The Alchemist (Jonson)
Alice in Wonderland
All My Sons
All Quiet on the Western
   Front
All the King's Men
All the Pretty Horses
The Ambassadors
American Beauty
Angela's Ashes
Animal Farm
Anna Karenina
Antigone
Antony and Cleopatra
Aristotle's Ethics
Aristotle's Poetics
Aristotle's Politics
As I Lay Dying
As You Like It
Astrophil and Stella
The Awakening
Babbitt
The Bacchae
Bartleby the Scrivener

The Bean Trees
The Bell Jar
Beloved
Benito Cereno
Beowulf
Bhagavad-Gita
Billy Budd
Black Boy
Bleak House
Bless Me, Ultima
The Bloody Chamber
Bluest Eye
The Bonfire of the
   Vanities
The Book of the Duchess
   and Other Poems
Brave New World
Breakfast at Tiffany's
Breakfast of Champions
The Brothers Karamazov
The Burning Plain and
   Other Stories
A Burnt-Out Case
By Night in Chile
Call of the Wild
Candide
The Canterbury Tales
Cat on a Hot Tin Roof
Cat's Cradle
Catch-22
The Catcher in the Rye
The Caucasian Chalk
   Circle
The Cherry Orchard
The Chocolate War
The Chosen

A Christmas Carol
Chronicle of a Death
   Foretold
Civil Disobedience
Civilization and Its
   Discontents
A Clockwork Orange
The Color of Water
The Color Purple
Comedy of Errors
Communist Manifesto
A Confederacy of
   Dunces
Confessions
Connecticut Yankee in
   King Arthur's Court
The Consolation of
   Philosophy
Coriolanus
The Count of Monte
   Cristo
Crime and Punishment
The Crucible
Cry, the Beloved
   Country
The Crying of Lot 49
Cymbeline
Daisy Miller
Death in Venice
Death of a Salesman
The Death of Ivan Ilych
Democracy in America
Devil in a Blue Dress
Dharma Bums
The Diary of a Young
   Girl by Anne Frank

For our full list of over 250 Study Guides, Quizzes,
Sample College Application Essays, Literature Essays and E-texts, visit:

www.gradesaver.com